True
Prayers

Lacey Whittaker

Trilogy Christian Publishers
A Wholly Owned Subsidiary of Trinity Broadcasting Network
2442 Michelle Drive
Tustin, CA 92780

Cover design by: Cornerstone Creative Solutions

For information, address Trilogy Christian Publishing
Rights Department, 2442 Michelle Drive, Tustin, Ca 92780.
Trilogy Christian Publishing/ TBN and colophon are trademarks of Trinity Broadcasting Network.

For information about special discounts for bulk purchases, please contact Trilogy Christian Publishing.

Manufactured in the United States of America

10 9 8 7 6 5 4 3 2 1

Library of Congress Cataloging-in-Publication Data is available.

ISBN 978-1-63769-166-3 (Print Book)
ISBN 978-1-63769-167-0 (ebook)

I would like to thank my wonderful, supportive team Justin, Addie, Liv, my amazing mother, Brenda, my sister, Lindsey, and Aunt Rita for encouraging me so much to go for it, stay with it, and keep it all about the one who created it!

In this book, you will find 167 True Prayers written with the Holy Spirit leading. You will read letters written about daily struggles and hope in our minds, flesh, spirit, wills and ways followed by scripture to align with God's word for us. These prayers will bring encouragement, guidance, peace, love and joy to each one willing to receive.

Lord, Your will is what we want. Your eyes to see. Your ears to hear. Your mouth to speak. We ask for all of this, Lord. We simply will not miss when our hearts are directed towards You. When our minds are focused on truth. Lord, give us all these things forever and ever. You will reign!

> "Thy kingdom come, Thy will be done in earth, as it is in heaven" (Matthew 6:10, KJV).

When you are lost and feel all alone, who do you call on the phone? Your mom? Your sister? Your friend? Well, let me tell you about my best friend! He is powerful and great! At night He will be there to put up any fight. He listens, comforts, and hears me through. He is more devoted than anyone. It's true!

> "And I will ask the Father and he will give you another Savior, the Holy Spirit of Truth, who will be to you a friend just like me" (John 14:16, TPT).

Tears are God's way of telling us it's ok to cry. It's ok to let go. It's ok to feel. It's ok to be known in His presence. It's ok to cry. Let those tears flow from your soul. Let them go deep into the great unknown. Let those tears flow heavily down your face. You, child, have a new name. Our Savior, He seeks these tears. He sees them and feels them everywhere. Child of the highest, let them flow. Release and you shall flow. Dump them into the deep blue sea. Oh, how your Father truly sees. Go now child, cry. It's ok! He will wipe them one sweet day.

> "Those who sow their tears as seeds will
> reap a harvest with joyful shouts of glee"
> (Psalm 126:5, TPT).

The day You came down from heaven to seek, to seek, to seek the lost. Oh, how I believe Your mighty ways are higher than a wave. I break, Father. Come down once again. Come down and see us win. Come down, Father, for I yearn for You. Come down, Father, and bring us back to true.

> "For the Son of Man has come to seek and to save that which was lost" (Luke 19:10, AMP).

Fear. What causes fear? Why do we long in fear? What makes us fear? What shakes us and leads us to death when we feel like we have nothing left? The enemy, the enemy, of course he comes and shakes and throws us off course by being sneaky. He may have his sneaky ways. We all know the games he plays. Being sneaky is no friend in my book. Being sneaky and sly with all those lies. Being sneaky and dark with no bark, Satan. Satan, you may think you won, but the King I serve is greater than anything you have done, so go down into the pits of hell where you belong. Watch me serve and worship my Lord all day long. With faith comes mighty, mighty control to kick you out and let go of this grip you hold on me. Oh, enemy don't you know, sneaky is a thief?

> "For God will never give you the spirit of fear, but the Holy Spirit who gives you mighty power, love, and self-control" (2 Timothy 1:7, TPT).

Dreams. Dreams are what you believe. Dreams, oh dreams can be heaven's army. Raining down for you to see in a different way. Can you believe these dreams, these dreams are heaven's hand to show you more? You can have these dreams. Ask for them. He will show you just like those parables of truth. These dreams, these dreams are life to me. They help me out when I need a key. A key to unlock the door. A key, oh they are so much more. Pay attention, I would say to your dreams. Ask the Holy Spirit to reveal and see, these dreams these dreams are a gift. Please, don't miss. Don't miss.

> "But there is a God in heaven who reveals secrets, and He has made known to King Nebuchadnezzar what will be in the latter days. Your dream, and the visions of your head upon your bed, were these" (Daniel 2:28, NKJV).

As he hung on that cross, could you imagine the sin, the sin that hung on that tree? The sin, the sin he took for you and me. The sin, the sin is gone away, so we could be free. Oh, that sweet day, how I wish, I wish I could see you. Then, to kiss your feet and love you until the end. The sin, the sin you paid, was bought for me to be free at any cost. As I see this sin on the cross, I see you Jesus, and I am no longer lost. Jesus, O Jesus, my precious friend. Jesus, oh, Jesus you called me to win. To defeat the enemy's schemes over me. To defeat and love my enemies. This sin, this sin, I do not see. This sin, this sin, nailed to a tree.

> "Broken and weeping, she covered his feet with the tears that fell from her face. She kept crying and drying his feet with her long hair. Over and over, she kissed Jesus' feet. Then she opened her flask and anointed his feet with her costly perfume as an act of worship" (Luke 7:38, TPT).

When I walk through the valley of the shadow of death, I shall fear no evil. Lord, I will fear no evil. You are with me. You are for me. You hold my right hand. No fire shall ever burn me. You will save me from the pits of hell. Father, may I never dwell there. Only in your arms. Only may I see Your Kingdom and how I was made to be free from sin. From life's tugs and tears, Father, I know You are with me everywhere.

> "Lord, even when your path takes me through the valley of deepest darkness, fear will never conquer me, for you already have! You remain close to me and lead me through it all the way. Your authority is my strength and my peace. The comfort of your love takes away my fear. I'll never be lonely, for you are near. You become my delicious feast even when my enemies dare to fight. You anoint me with the fragrance of your Holy Spirit; you give me all I can drink of you until my heart over-flows" (Psalm 23:4-5, TPT).

Do you fear? Do you worry? Are you anxious and insecure? I can say I know where to cast my cares. But sometimes the feelings overwhelm me and I can't get past them to see that we have a Savior who died to set us free. Lord, when I get lost this way, take my hand, pull me out and help me pray.

> "The angel of the Lord stooped down to listen as I prayed, encircling me, empowering me, and showing me how to escape. He will do this for everyone who fears God" (Psalm 34:7, TPT).

Locked, loaded, and ready to go. Jesus, all I desire is Your Holy Ghost flow. You are with me wherever I go. Hold me up. Place me there. Wipe away all my tears. As they fall, and as I fall apart, I know You hold them in Your heart. Jesus, O Jesus, You have come to set me free. Wash away all our inequities. It's Your face I seek. Wash them away so I can breathe.

> "For all of our faults and flaws are in full view to you. Everything we want to hide, you search out and expose by the radiance of your face" (Psalm 90:8, TPT).

Thank You, Jesus. You are so very true. All my devotion and honor are just for You. Keep me humble, keep me strong. This I know all along, You come to my defense. You come and win. You come to seek the lost. You come, oh, how we were bought. You come to save. You came and You gave. Your life was Yours to take. You came and gave. Thank You, Lord Jesus, I will always pray my faith stays high above the waves. I pray, oh, how I pray my faith stays high above the waves. You come, You seek the weak like me. I will forever be grateful for this seat. This seat, this seat I sit and see eternity. On my knees, forever grateful I will be as I seek, I seek eternity.

> "And God our Father will receive all the glory and the honor throughout the eternity of eternities! Amen!" (Philippians 4:20, TPT).

Children. Children. Children of God. You have been called, called, called. Children. Children. Children of God. You have been called, called, called for a higher purpose than this. Child. Child please don't miss His presence. His direction. His will, you see, is everything, everything to me. Now, go forth, a new day is ahead. Rest, oh, rest your head on His chest. Lay those worries, those cares, lay them there. He has come; He has sent all the best for His children. Now go rest in the presence of our Holy One. He sees everything. Go rest in the presence of our Holy One. Rest in His ways. His heart is pure, His burdens are light. He will be the one putting up the fight. You only need to be still in the presence of our holy one. Rest there chosen one.

> "Simply join your life with mine. Learn my ways and you'll discover that I'm gentle, humble, easy to please. You will find refreshment and rest in me" (Matthew 11:29, TPT).

When life gets hard, who will you run to? Will you run to the world or stay true to Him, the only one who can take away our sins? Who will you run to? Who will you run to? Who will you run to when life gets hard? This world is oh so dark. Run to Him, the Father, our King. Run to Him and simply believe. He can take on anything. Run to Him sweet child. Run to Him and see He holds the highest victory. Run to Him now. Run to Him and bow before the King of Kings, the Holy of Holies, the only one worthy of our praise. This life is short. Simply put your trust in Him. He will never leave or forsake you. He will go before you, always and forever, until the very end. Go child, find some rest. Your Father loves and knows you the best.

> "Trust in the Lord completely, and do not rely on your own opinions. With all your heart rely on him to guide you, and he will lead you in every decision you make" (Proverbs 3:5, TPT).

Light and salt, you are my light. The light for all the world to see. You are my light. Go out there and believe. The light of this world has come against all this petty and nonsense. Go out my children. Be the light and salt the flavor that doesn't bow down to the cost of this dark, cold world. You are my salt and light forever more. Go out. Go out. Be led by me. Go out. Go out and know you are in victory. Go out. Go out. Go out and see that you, my chosen, are set before thee.

"Your lives are like salt among the people. But if you, like salt, become bland, how can your 'saltiness' be restored? Flavorless salt is good for nothing and will be thrown out and trampled on by others. "Your lives light up the world. Let others see your light from a distance, for how can you hide a city that stands on a hilltop? And who would light a lamp and then hide it in an obscure place? Instead, it's placed where everyone in the house can benefit from its light. So, don't hide your light! Let it shine brightly before others, so that the commendable things you do will shine as light upon them, and then they will give their praise to your Father in heaven" (Matthew 5:13-16, TPT).

Loving, kind, merciful, all the days of my life. Open up like a book. Prosperous in all you do. Share me with everything you have. Hope as big as the sky, and faith as big as a comet. Hear what I say and say what I command. Goodness and mercy will follow you all the days of your life. Walk and abide in me. Through me there are heavenly rewards. Keep doing the right things. The right things will bring you to me. Keep going into the deep. The deep is where you learn and grow. Keep talking the talk. The talk is where you teach and speak. Keep listening. Listen with ears wide open. That's where you are humbled and secure. Always be secure in me for that's where your holiness and glory will fall. Always love. Love covers a multitude of sins. Always give. Giving is where your heart lies in me. Always have a faithful heart. Your faithful heart leads to desiring me. Always be pure. Your pureness shows strength and holiness. Always give your hand in need. Your hand shows work done by the Father. Always show gratitude, for that means you will inherit so much more. Always walk in humility, for where your heart lies, I lie. Lie down in a pasture with your head bowed and legs flat, soaking in the sun and glory on your skin. Engaging in the fruits and peace that only your father can give. Lie down and graze there, for you have been faithful, and rest in me. Rest in me. Thankful, humble hearts seek the Kingdom of God, and my throne that sits before my Father. That's a good place to be. Always strive to be there. You will never regret striving to be with your loving Father. Now go lie down and rest.

> "The Lord is my best friend and my shepherd. I always have more than enough. He offers a resting place for me in his luxurious love. His tracks take me to an oasis of peace, the quiet brook of bliss. That's where he restores and revives my life. He opens before me pathways to God's pleasure and leads me along in his footsteps of righteousness so that I can bring honor to his name. Lord, even when your path takes me through the valley of deepest darkness, fear will never conquer me, for you already have! You remain close to me and lead me through it all the way. Your authority is my strength and my peace. The comfort of your love takes away my fear. I'll never be lonely, for you are near. You become my delicious feast even when my enemies dare to fight. You anoint me with the fragrance of your Holy Spirit; you give me all I can drink of you until my heart overflows. So why would I fear the future? For your goodness and love pursue me all the days of my life. Then afterward, when my life is through, I'll return to your glorious presence to be forever with you!" (Psalm 23, TPT)

Highs and lows. All the subtle blows that come and go. One thing I know is my Father endured them all, nothing too big or too small. He suffered, died, and was buried. Rose again three days later. Walking this earth was no pleasure. He was an outcast to many. Spit on and beaten. Father, how I seek to be humble and pure. When I endure, oh how I want to be your everything, and be so holy and true, walking this earth like you do. Thank you, Father, for I have sinned. Now I will go and repent.

> "And anyone who comes to me must be willing to share my cross and experience it as his own, or he cannot be considered to be my disciple" (Luke 14:27, TPT)

Thankful heart, thankful mind. Thankful You are so loving, kind, and gracious. You are gracious, and You will always be gracious. Your plan has been for me, Father. Father help us see what You have to prosper, thee. Call us out, send us down. Forever walk and be found. Show us kingdoms and heavenly places. Show us, take us. Reign in the high spaces. Forever we seek these beautiful things; forever we seek You loving thee.

> "For it was only through this wonderful grace that we believed in him. Nothing we did could ever earn this salvation, for it was the gracious gift from God that brought us to Christ!" (Ephesians 2:8, TPT)

Scream and shout. I'm about all my Father's business He brings about. Show me Lord, show me what to do. My life is a sacrifice to You. I want to lead. I want to obey. Please, Lord, help me never to stray out of Your loving arms, out of Your will, Father. Show me how I can forever be still in the presence of my King. In the presence shall I sing, forever will I glorify Thee. Father, O Father, help me see.

> "Beloved friends, what should be our proper response to God's marvelous mercies? I encourage you to surrender yourselves to God to be his sacred, living sacrifices. And live in holiness, experiencing all that delights his heart. For this becomes your genuine expression of worship" (Romans 12:1, TPT)

I will follow, I will submit. Father, may I never miss the will You have for me. The price You paid for eternity is everything. Father show me mercy all my days. I will forever praise Your name and hold You dear. Father make it clear, for I never want to disappoint. Help me, Father. Help me see this is all for You, not me. When I get selfish or run scared, wake me up and show me You care. Take me from my flesh. Hold me until there's nothing left. Give me the grace I need to live in this world, but always serve Thee.

> "Serve and worship the awe-inspiring God. Recognize his greatness and bow before him, trembling with reverence in his presence" (Psalm 2:11, TPT).

I think about the children You gave me, how much I love them, and how You love me. I can't get past this creation, You see. I'm forever grateful You gave them to me, for I know they are Yours. Help me, Father. Help raise them to be pure, holy, and to see Your light. Guide them, Father. They are my heart's delight. Thank You, Father, for giving me them. The greatest blessing heaven sent.

> "For then you will be seen as innocent, faultless, and pure children of God, even though you live in the midst of a brutal and perverse culture. For you will appear among them as shining lights in the universe" (Philippians 2:15, TPT).

Rest, oh, rest. How You called us to rest. How we love Your sweet, satisfying rest. It takes our breath away, as we lay in Your abundant peace. How free we are, to be what You called us to be. You made us to rest in your purpose, in Your plan. In our lives, may we spend every day in the almighty rest of our Father. Thank You for rest. Thank You for peace. Thank You, Father, for loving and adoring me. Jesus. Jesus. Jesus. Your rest I can only find when I lay all my cares behind. May I forever believe in this rest You give so freely.

> "He offers a resting place for me in his luxurious love. His tracks take me to an oasis of peace, the quiet brook of bliss" (Psalm 23:2, TPT)

All the glory you could have missed. All the glory that comes from Him. All the glory that falls. All the glory, oh, how far it will run, how high it will go. This glory will never falter, but always show, the King of Kings in heavenly places. The King of Kings trading places with us. His children one day, we will see all the glory in his face. Until then, let it fall. Until then, I will forever call on You, Jesus. That day, oh, that day when I meet glory face to face.

> "So my Father, restore me back to the glory that we shared together when we were face-to-face before the universe was created" (John 17:5, TPT).

Peace I give to you. Take my peace and run. Peace I give to you. You only need to be still. This peace I freely give, for you to freely receive. This peace is life, the rest is death. Come take this peace. I have given you this peace for each day. Take this peace, this peace I give. Take this peace, and freely live. Take this peace and give. Take this peace, now take this peace. Bow to the Holy of Holies and remember how this peace comes and floods. Take this peace, I say, take this peace and stay. Take this peace and run. Take this peace and be undone. Take this peace, I say, let the rest fade away. Take this peace and go. Take this peace and show. Take this peace, I say, take this peace and lay. Take this peace, it's for you. Take this peace and stay in truth. Take this peace, now take this peace and bow. Take this peace my chosen ones. Take this peace and run. Take this peace, I say, take this peace and stay. Take this peace now, take this peace and bow. Take this peace, I freely give. Take it, have it, it's yours to live.

> "Then Jesus said, "I am light to the world and those who embrace me will experience life-giving light, and they will never walk in darkness" (John 8:12, TPT)

Lord, how do we fight the enemy? This fight, this fight won't go without a show. This enemy coming for you, this enemy coming for true, is a tiring beast that, when left to me, will no longer be able to take from thee. Go out there, fight his attacks, and win. Child know I already took care of him. His words and threats are worthless, and he knows child, oh child, if you only knew how much power you hold, you could take him down right when he came for you. Take him down. I will show you. Now, go put on the armor, and see how well it is to fight with me.

> "Embrace the power of salvation's full deliverance, like a helmet to protect your thoughts from lies. And take the mighty razor-sharp Spirit-sword of the spoken Word of God. Pray passionately in the Spirit, as you constantly intercede with every form of prayer at all times. Pray the blessings of God upon all his believers. Put on truth as a belt to strengthen you to stand in triumph. Put on holiness as the protective armor that covers your heart. Stand on your feet alert, then you'll always be ready to share the blessings of peace. In every battle, take faith

as your wrap-around shield, for it is able to extinguish the blazing arrows coming at you from the Evil One!" (Ephesians 6:14-18, TPT).

A kiss from heaven. Jesus, You are a kiss from what seems so far. Jesus, You came down to show us life and love, and never walk down this road alone, Father. Father, Your hand we shall hold open. Our eyes to see, our ears to hear. Father, You are our everything, so sweet, so nearby. With You by my side, whom shall, I fear. All my days are aligned.

Father a kiss from heaven is all I seek.

Pour Your Spirit out upon me. Anoint me with Your fire. You are my only one true desire. Pour it out, pour it out. You're all I'm about. Pour it on me. The evidence is seen. It's seen on my life, yes. Yes, pour the fire, the anointing, so I can be a walking, talking Jesus loving disciple, You have called me to be. Pour it out, pour that fire upon. Your victory has won.

> "I indeed baptize you with water unto repentance: but he that cometh after me is mightier than I, whose shoes I am not worthy to bear: he shall baptize you with the Holy Ghost, and with fire" (Matthew 3:11, KJV).

I am unconcerned and free of worry. Unconcerned and free of worry. Unconcerned and free of worry. I will lay down my fears and anxieties and put all my trust, hope, and will in You. I will lay down my anxieties and walk in peace. Feel the peace, the peace You give. The peace You share I will hold onto and declare, You, are Lord over my life, and I do not have to fight. Only be still and turn those worries into wills. Lord, You grant me peace to have all my days, I need not to ask. You give me peace; this I shall seek. You give me peace; this I shall leave. You give me peace, Your peace I have. This is all while my heart will be glad.

> "All the days of the afflicted are bad, But a glad heart has a continual feast [regardless of the circumstances]" (Proverbs 15:15, AMP)

No stress, you are blessed. No stress, you are blessed. No stress, you are blessed. No stress, you are blessed. No stress, you are blessed. No stress, you are blessed. No stress, you are blessed. No stress, you are blessed. Agreeable, delightful, good, enjoyable, grateful, heavenly, held high in reverence, worship, and honor.

I will leave the stress and only live blessed.

Hope, security, and love. All these things we dream of. Where shall we find these things? Not in this world, but in the heavenly place. Father open our eyes and mind to see what's important is the least of these. Open our hearts to hear Your words ever so clear. Make the dark days disappear, as our hope is set on You, we find the everlasting truth. Father help us see that this world is fading so vastly. May we keep our eyes on things above, may we see past all these earthly things shown with no love. May we seek the Kingdom above all things, Father, show us Your smiling face.

> "We have this certain hope like a strong, unbreakable anchor holding our souls to God himself. Our anchor of hope is fastened to the mercy seat which sits in the heavenly realm beyond the sacred threshold" (Hebrews 6:19, TPT).

Letting go of others. Letting go of our past. Letting go of these masks we hide behind because we don't want to show the world our dark cries. Letting go of what should've been. Letting go and releasing a grin, a grin, a grin you see, is the depth of faith we have for Thee. Letting go you see; we will live now only to be seen. To be seen so free, so free, so free, as the birds fly and the weather draws, we have no fear too big or too small, that our Father can't cure for us all.

Father help us to let go and release.

This feast. This feast. I graze, I eat this feast. This feast is life to me. This feast, this word You give to me, this feast, this feast is my everything.

> "Yes, feast on all the treasures of the heavenly realm and fill your thoughts with heavenly realities, and not with the distractions of the natural realm" (Colossians 3:2, TPT).

You are my helper, my friend, the one who comforts and knows no end. You are my joy, my light, the one who always provides. You are my shelter when I need to hide. You are my forever lifted high. You are my everything inside of me. You are the air I breathe. Thank You, Holy Spirit, for finding a home in me. Thank You, Father, for I cannot imagine life without Thee.

> "But when the Father sends the Spirit of Holiness, the One like me who sets you free, he will teach you all things in my name. And he will inspire you to remember every word that I've told you" (John 14:26, TPT).

You broke the bondages and religion I was in. You break the up bringing I was taught. You break them now, and no longer will I walk in the rituals I once believed. Father, You broke those burdens off me. Father, when they creep up again, please remind me it's not a sin, but Your will for me, Your will to see me set free.

> "So God brought out his chosen ones with singing; with a joyful shout they were set free!" (Psalm 105:43, TPT).

My heart is golden and pure, my heart is love and secure. My heart awakens the sick, my heart is love in all of it. My heart is spoken and true, my heart loves and adores You. My heart has never been so proud, as the day You called me from the clouds. My heart is forever beating for You; my heart holds forever truth. My heart is set above all things; my heart is here and rings.

> "My heart explodes with praise to you!
> Now and forever my heart bows in wor-
> ship to you, my King and my God!"
> (Psalm 145:1, TPT).

Where does sickness come from, I ask? Where does it go? When will I be healed? When I know like I know, the Holy Spirit inside of me could instantly heal me in one breath. I believe healing comes in a second. A miracle, in a thought, in a moment, in a day, in a week, in a lifetime. God's time is when healing comes. I will always believe healing will come because, what I know is, I have a Father who will heal, who loves to heal His children. Jehovah-Rapha, healing is the will of God, so I will forever say the praise of His name. He will heal; He will deliver on time. His time, His place. His name always and forever. That's my faith.

> "Then Jesus put his hands over their eyes and said, "You will have what your faith expects!" (Matthew 9:29, TPT).

Why do we fear? Why do we run? Why do we fall apart and say I'm done? Why do we fall into this pit, Father? Father, why is this? Why is it so hard to stay so strong? Is it because we depend on ourselves? Is that where we go wrong? Father, please lead. I need you forever to hold my peace.

> "Don't be pulled in different directions or worried about a thing. Be saturated in prayer throughout each day, offering your faith-filled requests before God with overflowing gratitude. Tell him every detail of your life" (Philippians 4:6, TPT).

Lord Jesus, Holy Spirit, please come give me comfort, peace, joy, patience, self-control, mercy, and grace all my days. I love and need You every second of every minute. Teach me to bow and be still in Your presence. Teach me to love and have grace and peace in the unknown. Teach me, show me, teach me, show me, teach me, show me. I love You, Lord. I love You. You are holy and good. Holy and true. I want to devote my never-ending life to You. Take it, have it and see, I will only honor Thee. I love Your grace and peace; I love You. You are everything to me. So holy and pure, a sacred friendship I adore. Teach me Your ways, show me Your grace. Teach me to have faith that outweighs the burdens of my peace. Teach me, show me, teach me, love me. I adore You; I love truth. You are my God for all my days. Teach me to love, to stay in Your everlasting peace. Your faithfulness shall show; I will always be in Your know. Teach me Your paths of least resistance. Teach me how to love through it. Show me how growth can heal; show me how I can feel holy and pure in this dark cold world. Lord, show me, show me, show me Your peace I hold with everything.

> "My wonderful God, you are to be praised above all; teach me the power of your decrees!" (Psalm 119:12, TPT).

Where does hurt and pain come from? It's not from me, it's not from You. It's from an evil one who loves to come and take life. The battle is won, it's his defeat. When He comes back, take his knees.

> "But Jesus said, 'Go away, enemy! For the Scriptures say: Kneel before the Lord your God and worship only him.'" (Matthew 4:10, TPT).

Holy, be ye holy. Yield to the spirit, not the desires of your flesh. Walk away from sin. God is marking you. Stay the course, stay the path, do only what the good Lord will ask.

> "As you yield freely and fully to the dynamic life and power of the Holy Spirit, you will abandon the cravings of your self-life" (Galatians 5:16, TPT).

I feel like one minute you're up and one minute you're down, one minute you're walking on the clouds, the next minute you get hit in the gut. One thing I know is true, my honor and devotion will always be for You. Never will I let these days of trouble take me to my grave, instead I will forever sing Your praise. If I know anything, it's true, You are always so good, so good all my days. You are always so good. Nothing shall I fear, no I shall never boast, only in the hope of one day ready to soar into the arms of my loving Father. Into the loving arms of my Father, who sees me, who sees eternity and just then, oh how safe I will be. Until then, I will sing Your praise. Until then, I will shout Your name, King of Kings, mighty and true, all my love only for You. Until You come back and take me home, I will forever roll over these storms. This I know I say is true, You love me and I love You. All is good, all is fine, only when I seek and fix my eyes will I pass over these troubles that seek me. Oh Father, I bow and believe, You are here, You are there, You are simply everywhere. As I lay my head down to sleep, it's Your face I shall seek and reap.

> "In this you rejoice greatly, even though now for a little while, if necessary, you have been distressed by various trials" (1 Peter 1:6, AMP).

We finished, He is the victory, He is the prize. Our eyes are set above on the prize the only prize known to man who will give you peace, give you strength, give you mercy to endure all things. Our eyes remain on the prize as we walk out and walk on into the victory the Lord above has given us. The victory of Jesus Christ, His name above all names. We win, we win, we win, we win, we win, we win, children of God, we win, we grin, we win, we grin. It's all for Him, it's all for Him, it's all for the One who created us within. Go now in victory and believe He has come to set the captives free. Go now in celebration, we have won the race kingdom come. Go now in peace, rest in his presence and see He is the one who always held the key.

> "A true athlete will be disciplined in every respect, practicing constant self-control in order to win a laurel wreath that quickly withers. But we run our race to win a victor's crown that will last forever" (1 Corinthians 9:25, TPT).

All my days I need You. All my nights You ring so true. All my love and honor glorifies truth. Father teach me to let go and see it's only You when the world comes to shake. Stand me on the rock that never quakes, for I look for You to say my name, come it will all be okay.

> "But the true Shepherd walks right up to the gate, and because the gatekeeper knows who he is, he opens the gate to let him in. And the sheep recognize the voice of the true Shepherd, for he calls his own by name and leads them out, for they belong to him. And when he has brought out all his sheep, he walks ahead of them and they will follow him, for they are familiar with his voice" (John 10:4, TPT).

The dark nights You keep me safe. The brightest days I lie in faith. Father, O Father, I look to see. Father, O Father, You will never leave, for this I will be grateful for eternity. Father, O Father, never will I say I could do this alone with You at bay. I need You more than I could ever believe. Father, O Father, sit, stay and speak love over me.

> "No matter how bitterly the proud mockers speak against me, I refuse to budge from your precepts" (Psalm 119:51, TPT).

The path, the purpose, the plan You have for us brings us grace, brings us love. Show us Your will, Father, now show us more in our bow. May our ways be broken, as we know they are carnal. Your ways be spoken and all them to be followed. Father make clear Your will for our lives. Father make clear You are our true delight.

> "Guide me into the paths that please you, for I take delight in all that you say" (Psalm 119:35, TPT).

Where do you go to run and hide? Where do you go when your thoughts collide? Cry out to Him, the One who saves. Cry out and please don't wait. He has come to take away all the sins we portray. Cry out to Him, repent no more shame. Cry out, there will be a day no more cries, no more pain. He our great Father takes it all away. Until that day we see his face, cry out to the only one who gives us grace.

> "Yet when holy lovers of God cry out to him with all their hearts, the Lord will hear them and come to rescue them from all their troubles" (Psalm 34:17, TPT).

All these ups and downs, all the stops and turn arounds. All this, Father, we walk through, all this, Father, I could not do without Your sweet love and grace. Without your guidance, I would drift away into a deep hate. This world knows so well, Father, O Father, keep my eyes and heart straight geared towards the One who saved my soul. Geared towards the One who always knows. Geared toward You, Father, let me see, let me see how to walk in sweet everlasting victory.

> "If your faith remains strong, even while surrounded by life's difficulties, you will continue to experience the untold blessings of God! True happiness comes as you pass the test with faith, and receive the victorious crown of life promised to every lover of God!" (James 1:12, TPT).

Jesus died to set us free. Jesus died so we would believe. There is a greater reward in heaven than this. Take hold of this precious gift. He was born in a manager. He traveled and preached. He was born to save the lost, especially me. He was born to take away these sins that lead, that lead us into pits of hell not streams of living water. He proceeds to give us everything, Jesus, O Jesus, He came to save. Jesus oh help me to live everyday thanking you for all that You done, loving You and forever being undone. By Your pursuit of me, by this relationship we have. O Jesus, help my eyes to see this simple amazing gift given for me.

> "For this is how much God loved the world—he gave his one and only, unique Son as a gift. So now everyone who believes in him will never perish but experience everlasting life" (John 3:16, TPT).

Hope, love, peace, security, all these things we can reap. We can reap, we can reap when we sow these precious seeds it blesses you and blesses me. Sow, sow, sow, and reap all these good things that come from heaven above. Sow them now and reap a full harvest in due time, His time. Sow, sow, sow. Sow all the good things of the Lord and rest and see your reward.

> "And don't allow yourselves to be weary or disheartened in planting good seeds, for the season of reaping the wonderful harvest you've planted is coming!" (Galatians 6:9, TPT).

All these thoughts, all these things, they come and try to take the real thing. Slow them down, throw them out. You child were never to be about all these things he throws at you. All these things to make you stumble from truth. But you have a Father who loves and adores. You have a Father who speaks so much more. So, let him go see another day, let him go and be okay. Let him go into the deep pits of hell. Let him go and all will be well.

> "We can demolish every deceptive fan-
> tasy that opposes God and break through
> every arrogant attitude that is raised up
> in defiance of the true knowledge of
> God. We capture, like prisoners of war,
> every thought and insist that it bow in
> obedience to the Anointed One" (2
> Corinthians 10:5, TPT).

My eyes, my eyes perfect and true. My eyes, my eyes forever fixed on You. My eyes, my eyes have fully seen the gracious love of the Lord overflowing. My eyes, my eyes are fixed on the prize, the One above I hold so high. My eyes, my eyes may they never seek anything but my precious Savior looking at me.

> "Unto you I lift up my eyes, O You who are enthroned in the heavens!" (Psalm 123:1, AMP).

Let go, let go, let go, let go. Let go, let go all of your pain. Let go, let go at the mention of His name. Let go, let go and fully seek His wisdom. Oh, He loves and adores thee. Let go, let go of all the past hurt. Let go, let go child, know your worth. It was paid, oh, it was bought. Live like it free and holy! Go now, let go and see when we truly let go, we are all we can be. In peace, oh peace, help us let go. For when we see, we see with eyes for eternity.

> "All who seek to live apart from me will lose it all. But those who let go of their lives for my sake and surrender it all to me will discover true life!" (Matthew 10:39, TPT).

All these days that pass, they really go by too fast. All these days that pass, Father, I love You, please come back. These days are getting longer, Lord. We need You now even more. Father who one sweet day, Father I long to see Your face. Father, please come back. We are ready to see You take us back, take us to that heavenly place. Take us there where sickness cannot be feared, take us, show us what true love is. Take us now, we will forever live.

> "And He will wipe away every tear from their eyes; and there will no longer be death; there will no longer be sorrow and anguish, or crying, or pain; for the former order of things has passed away" (Revelation 21:4, AMP).

Come closer, walk close to Thee. Bow down, adore the King of Kings. He has come to give you life, and your breath will lead you to many steps. Bow in awe, bow in worship, bow in praise. It's only His face we will take. We will take it with us wherever we go, for we know how much power it holds. Bow down and worship our King, bow down and say I will honor Thee all my days. I will pursue You all my days. I will see the power of Your truth.

> "Come and kneel before this Creator-God; come and bow before the mighty God, our majestic maker!" (Psalm 95:6, TPT).

Prosper in all that you do. Lord, Your words are truth, day and night. I meditate on these words; they make me so strong. I hold on like a good child does. I hold on to all my Fathers love. Prosper in all that you do. It's simple, listen and read truth.

> "Do yourself a favor and love wisdom. Learn all you can, then watch your life flourish and prosper!" (Proverbs 19:8, TPT).

Father. When we fear Father, come and show us love. Show us peace. Show us what we were made to be. Conquer our past, conquer our fears. O Father please draw near. Never shall we fall into these pits. Never shall we ever call it quits. We know the one who is in control. We know the One who never grows cold. Father, O Father, must we forget. Wake us up and have us shift from the darkness. We are called into the light. Father, O Father, put up a fight.

> "Then Jesus said, "I am light to the world and those who embrace me will experience life-giving light, and they will never walk-in darkness" (John 8:12, TPT).

It's New Year's Day, and all I can do is pray, pray, pray. Pray for Your Kingdom come, your will be done, come shake and run. Your presence in this place. It's You we seek and You we praise. In all of our days, You hold true. In all of our days left to guide us, may we put You first in whatever we do. May we always stop to adore and glorify truth. Lord, take me by the hand this year. I only want Your plans, your will, Your way Father, O Father, it's only You I will take.

> "A new song for a new day rises up in me every time I think about how he breaks through for me! Ecstatic praise pours out of my mouth until everyone hears how God has set me free. Many will see his miracles; they'll stand in awe of God and fall in love with him!" (Psalm 40:3, TPT).

Another year has come and passed. It's Your presence I grasp. As we enter into a new year, let me hold all things You love so dear. As the days, months, and weeks ahead come, let me be filled even more with Your love. As I walk along this road, let Your story be the one that is told. Give me faith over fear, grace over condemnation. Let me praise You in both the high and low places. As we say goodbye, we say hello to another day with You on the throne, glorious in praise we shout Your great name.

> "So everyone, exalt the Lord our God facedown before his glory-throne, for he is great and holy" (Psalm 99:5, TPT).

When peace comes, it comes with peace. When dreams come, He leaves us with these. Come Holy Spirit, revive in me a secret place where I can dream. Come Holy Spirit, flood me with peace, give me more than I dare to believe. For I have known You came for me and to give me a life with abundant peace. For this is what my heart truly seeks, a life full of abundant peace. For this I live and receive a life full of abundant peace. Jesus, O Jesus, more than anything, give me life where freedom reigns. No control or thoughts that stray, just a life with You fully in praise.

> "Now, may the Lord himself, the Lord of peace, pour into you his peace in every circumstance and in every possible way. The Lord's tangible presence be with you all" (2 Thessalonians 3:16, TPT).

Fear and worry hold no real ground. All they do is make you run circles around. Look up child, there are spirits out there. Spirits that love nothing more than to tear you apart and drop you into a pit. Child look up and don't miss, don't miss the time to fight and say, "I do not want to live this way. I have a Father who has paid all these sins I dare not take." So, stand up against Satan and his evil ways. Fear, worry, you cannot stay.

> "Don't be pulled in different directions or worried about a thing. Be saturated in prayer throughout each day, offering your faith-filled requests before God with overflowing gratitude. Tell him every detail of your life" (Philippians 4:6, TPT).

Holy Spirit is three in one. Holy Spirit, receive and run, run, run. Holy Spirit guides and comforts you. Holy spirit shows you truth. Holy Spirit has been sent, so my chosen will always win. Holy Spirit is for you to reap. Holy Spirit comes, yippee! Holy Spirit is your friend in me. Holy Spirit, oh can you see? Holy Spirit will live within you. Holy Spirit will come and ring truth. Holy Spirit is truly your greatest gift. Holy Spirit is not a wish. Holy Spirit is your dearest friend, so treat the Holy Spirit better than man. Holy Spirit will guide and lead you. Holy Spirit will bring you truth. Depend on Him as you depend on Me, watch out and see, see, see.

> "And I will ask the Father and he will give you another Savior, the Holy Spirit of Truth, who will be to you a friend just like me—and he will never leave you. The world won't receive him because they can't see him or know him. But you know him intimately because he remains with you and will live inside you" (John 14:16-17, TPT).

Control. Where does it come from? Where does it live? I believe it comes from within, when we don't surrender, don't let go, don't let our Father be the one in the know. Control. It hurts, it causes pain, it knows no real name. Let go, let God take over and see, He has the best will for thee.

Let go and fully surrender your heart today.

Healing and truth. All these good things come from You. Heal us. Our broken hearts too. Heal us, take us, mend us up with You. Jesus, You are holy, holy, holy. Jesus, You are worthy, worthy, worthy. Jesus, come be by our side. Jesus, hold us throughout the dark nights. Stay by our side, keep us there, hold us tight. With You, we will always stay, with You, life will be ok. Lord Jesus, You are truth. Lord Jesus, show us You. Show us Your light that guides our nights. Show us, be there, sleep right beside.

> "Finally, beloved friends, be cheerful! Repair whatever is broken among you, as your hearts are being knit together in perfect unity. Live continually in peace, and God, the source of love and peace, will mingle with you" (2 Corinthians 13:11, TPT).

I know we win. I know we seek. I know we fall down to our knees. I know You are Lord. I know You are King. I know like I know. You are my everything. Father seek us out. Father show us what You are all about. As we turn our eyes fixed on You, Father come show us Your very truth. Your word is heard. Your word we seek. Father, we need this word. We are so weak without Your presence. Without our faith, we would be lost and shake, shake, shake. Help the lost find You. Help the lost and lead them to truth. Help the lost for they do not know what keys our heavenly Father holds. Seek them out, help them face their insecurities. When they know You hold it all, they will come and not fall.

> "There once was a shepherd with a hundred lambs, but one of his lambs wandered away and was lost. So the shepherd left the ninety-nine lambs out in the open field and searched in the wilderness for that one lost lamb. He didn't stop until he finally found it. With exuberant joy he raised it up and placed it on his shoulders, carrying it back with cheerful delight!" (Luke 15:4-5, TPT).

The sun, the sun, He gave for light. The sun, the sun, always a delight. The sun, the sun, so warm on our skin. The sun, the sun, you always win. You give, you give, oh the sun please come again.

> "The light is sweet and pleasant, and
> it is good for the eyes to see the sun"
> (Ecclesiastes 11:7, AMP).

Many trials and tribulations had come but, I kept walking through them all. By his grace, looking back now I see how He had always been walking with me. Healing would then take place. Life was back in an ordinary way. But as life came back and I was walking through, I had let the closeness stray and was not depending on You. So, more would come and more would stay until I finally woke up to say, "Jesus, You are my all and all my everything. This life I live is for You to take."

> "For it is not from man that we draw our life but from God as we are being joined to Jesus, the Anointed One. And now he is our God-given wisdom, our virtue, our holiness, and our redemption" (1 Corinthians 1:30, TPT).

It was that night I remember well. Sleep, oh sleep, I knew so well. I was up wide awake when I heard Him say, go, go, go and lay. So, on the couch I was staring in a gaze when He said, look, oh look, all that I gave. As He showed me a cross, I heard Him say, look, oh look, the blood that I gave. I love you this much, I love you this much. Look at this cross. I love you this much and after that day, something changed.

> "Keep in mind that we who belong to Jesus, the Anointed One, have already experienced crucifixion. For everything connected with our self-life was put to death on the cross and crucified with Messiah" (Galatians 5:24, TPT).

All the persecution I have felt means nothing to what You were dealt. Oh Jesus, open our eyes to see that when we get persecuted, we are really closer to Thee.

> "Although the believers were scattered by persecution, they preached the wonderful news of the word of God wherever they went" (Acts 8:4, TPT).

> "So that no one would be shaken by these persecutions, for you know that we are destined for this" (1 Thessalonians 3:3, TPT).

> "For all who choose to live godly as worshipers of Jesus, the Anointed One, will also experience persecution" (2 Timothy 3:12, TPT).

Days, months, and years had led me to more than tears. He took me through this life I had proceeded. He took me through all I had seen. He took me through to show me how to undo the past hurts and also the truths. That day, that day I chose to surrender and say, "Take it all Lord, it will be ok." That day, that day I remember well. That day, that day I stopped ringing my own bell. He took what I had and gave me even more. He took what I had, and I left it on the floor. He took what I had and blessed me even more. These gifts that I have seen, He showed me even more. I will forever hold on to and be grateful for more, more, more. You see all these gifts He has given has really helped me to see, to see I need them to be. To see, to see the spiritual is more than men, to see, to see all these gifts. To see that you can have life and more abundantly, let go surrender and see what He wants to give you is to be free.

> "Yet all of this was so that he would redeem and set free all those held hostage to the written law so that we would receive our freedom and a full legal adoption as his children" (Galatians 4:5, TPT).

One day a prophet came to me to say, "are you ready to go deeper? It's yours to take. Just believe and say, 'Jesus, I love you, you know everything.'" That day, I will always remember very well; that day, all else that mattered fell. That day, I knew I could have a real relationship with You; that day ever since I have been running after truth.

> "Be faithful to guard the sweet harmony of the Holy Spirit among you in the bonds of peace" (Ephesians 4:,3 TPT).

If I said it would be easy, I would be lying. If I said it wasn't hard, you would know I wasn't telling the truth. This life You have given me I have had to choose more ways than one. It's only You. Oh the grace You give when we follow You. This road I have walked could not be truer. To say that I am blessed would not do enough justice for You. This life I have now is everything, and oh, how I love to say Your sweet name. This life I have now is only You. This life I have now I will choose to love and honor You. This life that I have I will follow You. This life that I have will ring so true. It's not always easy that's surely the truth, but this life that I have I would never trade you.

> "Jesus replied, 'Listen to my words: anyone who leaves his home behind and chooses God's kingdom realm over wife, children, parents, and family, it will come back to him many more times in this lifetime. And in the age to come, he will inherit even more than that—he will inherit eternal life!'" (Luke 18:29-30, TPT).

The flow, the flow, the Holy Ghost flow. I long to forever hold the flow that keeps my soul at peace. The flow that leaves me secure and pleased. The flow that will turn tables to truth. The flow that teaches me all about you. The flow, the flow, the Holy Ghost flow. Oh, how I long wherever you go.

> "Believe in me so that rivers of living water will burst out from within you, flowing from your innermost being, just like the Scripture says!" (John 7:38, TPT)

I am focused on your face. I am living by your grace. I am loved and adored. I am your child and so much more. You have given me so much more; my eyes simply don't see. Father, O Father, let it be your face. The only one I seek all day with praise and thanksgiving.

> "Make Your face shine upon Your servant; Save me in Your lovingkindness"
> (Psalm 31:16, AMP).

I journal. I write. It gives me peace at night when my fight has been strong, when my will has been long. Father, I look solely to You for strength to pull through. Lord, our eyes only on truth. That's the only way I know I will get through is You.

> "But he answered me, 'My grace is always more than enough for you, and my power finds its full expression through your weakness.' So I will celebrate my weaknesses, for when I'm weak I sense more deeply the mighty power of Christ living in me" (2 Corinthians 12:9, TPT"

Distraction. Distraction. That's how the enemy wants us to be, distracted. Oh, distracted. How he fights to keep us there, to live in a world that doesn't care, when our focus shifts from You to him, Jesus take us back in. You will always win.

> "We look away from the natural realm and we fasten our gaze onto Jesus who birthed faith within us and who leads us forward into faith's perfection. His example is this: Because his heart was focused on the joy of knowing that you would be his, he endured the agony of the cross and conquered its humiliation, and now sits exalted at the right hand of the throne of God!" (Hebrews 12:2, TPT).

Power, power, power of the resurrected King. Power we hold inside thee when we come and let that power live. Oh, how lives will be changed from within this power. This power, the greatest one I know, take my life, so I may live and show this power. This power, this power inside me makes all those devils turn and flee. This power, this power that lives inside me, it's available to anyone who believes.

> "Rise up and put your might on display!
> By your strength we will sing and praise
> your glorious power!" (Psalm 21:13,
> TPT).

One thing I know is true: You gave me life and a choice to choose. You gave me my own choices, Father. Help me to follow You all my days. Help me never to look back and say, "Wow, where did I turn away." Father, O Father, I will always pray for You to be right by my side, for You to show delight, for You to see the fire inside, love that burns all through the night and during my darkest days. Father, O Father, I know You will never leave me to stray.

> "Then Peter and the apostles replied, 'We must obey God rather than men [we have no other choice]'" (Acts 5:29, AMP).

Where does distraction come from? My mind keeps spinning around and around. I can't focus. I'm in a fog. I believe the enemy comes like a thief. He comes with lies to make you believe, and one day you wake up and see everything that was, is not to be. I believe he comes in our thoughts. He comes and tries to take what was bought. I believe in sweet victory and the enemy has no real hold on me. So, I rise up and pray and, to you enemy, you simply cannot stay. Bye, oh see you. You go now and leave me alone. I have a God who knows, and you have no part here to show. So, flee, flee, flee and leave. Go back to hell and see that you may try to come and take but you will never have my namesake.

> "With God's help we will fight like heroes
> and he will trample down our every foe!"
> (Psalm 60:12, TPT).

People will come and shoot you down. They will try to hit you and never slow down. Lord, give us eyes to see our enemies as You see. May we let go and forgive. May we know this battle is within. The flesh is weak, but the spirit is strong. Lord, help us see when we are wrong. Keep our eyes and focus on You. Keep them there, that's truth. Let us trust You through and never let our flesh rule over You.

> "I'll always have an answer for those who
> mock me because I trust in your word"
> (Psalm 119:42, TPT).

When life gets hard and shoots you down. When people come and cut you with a frown. When you get knocked down and back up again. Child look up. You win, you win, you win. Jesus loves you. You win, you win with truth. Next time someone comes knocking at your door, stand up, look up and roar, roar, roar.

> "I look up to the mountains and hills, longing for God's help. But then I realize that our true help and protection come only from the Lord, our Creator who made the heavens and the earth" (Psalm 121:1-2, TPT)

Focus, love, strength, all these things at our Fathers name. O Abba, how I love to praise all these things at the mention of Your name. The dead will rise, the sick will be healed, Your love for us goes deeper than we could feel. Father show us all these good things. Touch us, bring honor and glory and praise. Father seek us where we are at. Father, You know we love to chat. Father, Your will over ours. Father, we love that smile. Father show us love and faith and strength. Show us now. Let us be forever found in love and grace. Father, O Father, we are here to stay. Father O Father, come and take.

> "He prayed, 'Abba, my Father, all things are possible for you. Please—don't allow me to drink this cup of suffering! Yet what I want is not important, for I only desire to fulfill your plan for me'" (Mark 14:36, TPT).

Hope, love, peace, affliction of these. The enemy loves to come and take everything you were given. That's his ways. O Father, I pray he knows not to come to this child to take. He goes away by the sound of our praise to the only One who saves. To the only One who stays. Father, O Father, one sweet day we can lay to rest and only hear Your name.

> "In all of my affliction I find great comfort in your promises, for they have kept me alive!" (Psalm 119:50, TPT).

What does finishing strong look like to you? To me it looks like a bent tree leaning over, looking to die, but look out, watch out. Here comes the sky, a ray of sunshine hits and pushes you through till the end. Never give up, never give in, with Jesus as our guide, we will always win and never die.

> "So if the tree is good, it will produce good fruit; but if the tree is bad, it will bear only rotten fruit and it deserves to be cut down and burned" (Matthew 7:17-19, TPT).

Highs and lows, the depths of my soul. You are raining down, blessing the only thing I know. Father, it's Your favor I seek. It's Your wisdom for eternity with these that fall afresh on my soul. I will keep holding on. Don't you know this is what I live for. Only you to say when she is gone, she always obeyed.

> "Yes, this is God's generous reward for those who love him" (Psalm 128:4, TPT).

Lord, why I ask? Why sickness and disease? Why all these such things? I know You have a purpose and plan I don't see, but why, oh why, do we see these evil things? Help us walk through and understand. Help us see the greater purpose and plan, Lord. When we are weary and tired too. Help us see only You.

> "A person may have many ideas concerning God's plan for his life, but only the designs of his purpose will succeed in the end" (Proverbs 19:21, TPT).

Where do you hold all your cares? Do you tuck them in, hide them down into a deep pit? Do you stuff them and keep them there until one day you can't hold another care? Child of God, don't you know child of God, it's not yours to hold. Release them now, release, release in your bow. The enemy loves to keep this grip on you. Release, release and run to truth.

> "Casting all your cares [all your anxieties, all your worries, and all your concerns, once and for all] on Him, for He cares about you [with deepest affection, and watches over you very carefully]" (1 Peter 5:7, AMP).

Father, O Father, as You smile down from above, I feel the smile reaching so gently. I'm so loved. When I walk away from You, I am called back and further promise truth all my days. You are here to stay all my days. Take me further away from what this world offers me, Father, O Father, it's only You I seek.

> "Seek the LORD and His strength; Seek His face continually [longing to be in His presence]" (1 Chronicles 16:11, AMP).

Our mind is a battlefield. One that the enemy loves to take. He loves to place a thought and try to make it stay but then the word shows up and I meditate on all the good things of the Lord that makes me so strong. So devil, you hold no real ground. The mention of His name makes you run back into the ground. So, next time you come knocking me down, turnaround. This child of God does not mess around.

> "For God did not give us a spirit of timidity or cowardice or fear, but [He has given us a spirit] of power and of love and of sound judgment and personal discipline [abilities that result in a calm, well-balanced mind and self-control]" (2 Timothy 1:7, AMP).

When the days get long and come to an end. When tomorrow you wake and it looks no different. When you have the hope and faith to take another step, but the time is looking gray. When you look back and only see the pain. When all those days you sit feeling defeat, Lord, when will all be great again and I can think, He comes down and whispers close, "daughter, oh daughter, I never let go. Soon, oh soon, victory you see growth is for you and it's for me."

> "So then, my soul, why would you be depressed? Why would you sink into despair? Just keep hoping and waiting on God, your Savior. For no matter what, I will still sing with praise, for living before his face is my saving grace!" (Psalm 42:5, TPT).

Lord, God, Holy One, You are far above anything I could ever seek. You are the best for me.

> "Shout hallelujah to Yahweh! May every one of his lovers hear my passionate praise to him, even among the council of the holy ones" (Psalm 111:1, TPT).

When the nights are long, and the days are short. When we feel we are running off course. Come to us and whisper here, calm us from every fear, Lord. We know You have won. We know the battle is won. We know the truth, Father. When the enemy comes, and we choose. Father come help us from our doubt. We will always know what You're about, Father. Don't let us stay any longer there. Pull us out in the midnights air.

> "And He said, 'Why are you troubled, and why are doubts rising in your hearts?'" (Luke 24:38, AMP).

Do you ever wonder why things happened? Do you ever wonder where God is? When something is pulling and tugging you, trying to take you into a dark place of hate, of insecurity? Do you ever wonder, oh do you ever wonder why? I do. I wonder why when life is fine one minute and the next you get hit like a side wipe, like a slap and punch where did you even come from? Jesus came and probably wondered these things too. He came from heaven and walked the walk of faith. Oh, how I yearn to have the faith and strength Jesus had when He walked here. Oh, how I could bear more, let go more, forgive more, respond more humbly. Oh, how I seek to walk as Jesus walked. Oh, how deep down in my soul I hope I can walk like Jesus walked. What an honor to know Thee. What an honor to be loved by Thee. Please help when times get hard to not just fall apart but run to the loving arms of our Father and not ask why, but say, "Lord, I will walk through this valley, through this fight, through this persecution, if You will walk with me right beside."

> "Therefore as you have received Christ Jesus the Lord, walk in [union with] Him [reflecting His character in the things you do and say—living lives that lead others away from sin]" (Colossians 2:6, AMP).

When you're running a race, you feel like stopping or giving up. When you're running a race, you feel like there's nothing left to run to, get to the end to finish strong. You need Gods love, His hand in the race to push you through, to look and say, "I am so proud of you." Just a little while longer now, before long, you will be finished and wow what a day to finish strong. Hold on, He will move you further along. Hold on, there is purpose in the pain. Hold on, He is giving you new reins. With pain comes growth, everyone knows. Hold on, hold steady, hold deep, it will be over, and you will reap.

> "I run straight for the divine invitation
> of reaching the heavenly goal and gaining
> the victory-prize through the anointing
> of Jesus" (Philippians 3:14, TPT).

Letting go means freedom. Letting go means joy, peace, love, and everything your Father sends from above. To let go means you trust in Me, believe Me, love Me, adore Me, give your worries and concerns to Me. You give them all to Me and in that, you will have an everlasting rest that no one can out do. This, my child, I have given to you. So, rest, rest and know your Father is always here to show kindness, love and truth and all my devotion to you.

"For My yoke is easy [to bear] and My burden is light" (Matthew 11:30, AMP).

How I met Jesus:

This would be a road I've walked on for many years. I felt Him tugging but would never draw near, until one day cancer was on my name. Until one day, panic had led me to say Jesus, O Jesus, O Jesus, how I need You, Jesus. O Jesus show me You are true. "Jesus, O Jesus" is all I could say. Jesus, O Jesus would You come and stay. Jesus, O Jesus I surely need you. Jesus, O Jesus just show me the real You. Jesus, O Jesus my heart is crying out. I have nowhere else to turn and need You right now. Jesus, O Jesus the peace You would bring was more, more, more than anything. I knew right then when Jesus was all I could say that You were the one who would save, save, save, oh save me from all my failures and make me believe that nothing in this world could compare to You, Jesus. Eternity is right here for when I call on Your name. You are so near.

Jesus, Jesus, Jesus.

Life comes and life goes. One day you are here, the next day you're not. How will you live your time here on earth? Will you make a difference in other people's lives? Will you show love to the unlovable? Will you speak kindly to the ones who hurt you? Will you go after that one lost soul if it means you have to count the cost before you? What will you choose? Jesus died for us to live with a purpose, with love, with grace, with mercy at His name. So, how will you live knowing He died to give you life? Will you live to please our Creator or man? I struggle with both. On one side, it's so easy to say yes to the Lord, and a moment later it's so easy to say yes to man. What I have learned is, pleasing man will never fulfill my purpose here on earth. Only the love and obedience I have with Christ fulfills my purpose. So, I will ask today who will you serve? We have one life here and I want to live it fully for the One who created me to be here, amen.

Who will you serve?

You are with me. Never will You leave me. You guide me, provide for me, keep me strong and faithful and true. Holy are You my King. Holy You are and will always be. I will walk this life never complete without You living inside me Holy Spirit. You are welcome here. Never leave me, and I will not fear with You leading me, guiding me all my days. Wow, a leap of faith is all You need to believe in eternity, eternity, eternity. One day we shall be living in eternity with You, all powerful one, You Father, Son, and Holy Ghost. I sure love You, Holy Ghost. You speak so much truth, Holy Ghost. You are what we need. You are our everything. Help us get this, receive this, without You we simply cannot live.

> "Now, the 'Lord' I'm referring to is the Holy Spirit, and wherever he is Lord, there is freedom" (2 Corinthians 3:17, TPT).

Sometimes you win. Sometimes you lose. Sometimes you laugh. Sometimes you cry. Sometimes you want to scream. Sometimes you stay in peace. I have learned that things come and things go in this life. Rarely are they fair in the world. When you follow, follow the One who gives you life. Follow the One who gives you light life more abundantly. Yes, you have a choice to soak or see pity or shake. Life's not fair but it's ok when you see the One who created you. When you feel the love He has for you, it will get you through the hard times. I will follow, follow, follow as long as I live here. To show the truth I have and honor for You, the only One who matters. And eternity shall I forever seek what happens to me in this world I can bear when my eyes are fixed on my Father up there.

The seasons of life we can bear, when we keep our eyes on the One who cares.

Rest, oh how I love Your rest. The rest is like nothing I have ever known. It makes me lay down in a field of peace forever while I sleep. Oh, but sleep is not only rest. It's when you have been put to the test, when your soul is tired and weary. You know, it's when you have had enough, come undone, and then you sit and seek Thee and He whispers so softly, "child, oh child, all is alright. Come stay with me, and I will fight. You only need to be still. You only need my will, so child, oh child rest in my loving arms." You don't always have to be so strong. Surrender, surrender, surrender now, all those burdens that carry you around. Now go, rest, rest, rest into the deep. Oh, how when I rest it brings me so much peace.

Be still and rest.

As I lay here tonight, I can only dream of what it may be like on that day I see Your face. O Jesus, I simply cannot wait to worship You all my days. O Jesus, I simply cannot wait to lock eyes with You at those pearly gates. May we sit a lifetime and never see as much glory as when we see our King.

Only shall I yearn to seek Your face.

Father, O Father, it's come to this. I need You now. Please come quick. I call for You. I call and repent. Forgive me, Father, from all my sins. The cross You bore takes them away. The cross You bore will never fade as we grow old. Let us never forget the day You left heaven to take care of all of it. Let my heart always be grateful. For this, O Father, help me never forget. For if You never took on that cross, we would all be forever lost.

The cross You bore took our sins forevermore.

This world is crazy. This world is fake. This world has come to take the name of Jesus out of it, you see. The name of Jesus, spread His name everywhere you go. Spread his name and show, show, show the light living inside you. You see, will be shared for eternity. Go now, share the light. Go now, make this world bright. Go now, His Kingdom is at hand. Go now, He has the bigger plan. Go now, seek Him on your knees. Go now and truly believe that the King of the world reigns to see so much more glory and peace. Go now, seek Him where you are at. Go now, that's that. Go now and see He has come to give life more abundant and free.

> "Let me be clear, the Anointed One has set us free—not partially, but completely and wonderfully free! We must always cherish this truth and stubbornly refuse to go back into the bondage of our past" (Galatians 5:1, TPT).

When life moves you, you ought to be still. When life pushes you, go to Him and be still. When life throws you down, look up and see the beauty of the Lord, His eyes on thee. He has come. He has sent. He has come to take care of all of it. Look to those eyes, keep them fixed there. Look to those eyes, all is well. Look to those eyes fixed and see He has come to set us free. Set us free from the evil and darkness here. Set us free from the worry of all our cares. Set us free from what our little eyes see. To set us free to live life fully. You see, go to Him in the soft whispers here. Go to Him child and do not fear. Go to Him and truly see He has you to hold for victory. This fight, this battle is already won. It died at the cross, so go be strong. It is well, oh well, oh well in your soul. It is well, it is well, it is well, you know. Go rest in the arms of Jesus. He keeps His chosen there. All the rest has to flee when we rest with Thee.

Rest in the precious Savior's arms.

When I walk through the valley, You are with me. When I am on the mountain top with great joy, You are with me. When I'm suffering and sick, You are with me. When I am lost and confused, You are with me. When I'm walking down a long dark road, You are with me. When I lay my head, You are with me. In the morning when I rise, You are with me. Never let me forget, You are with me always and forever. Never will You leave me. Never will You forsake me, even when my eyes don't see. I know You see what's ahead of me. You have planned it for my purpose for a time as this I simply won't miss when I look to You. Look to truth. I will gaze into the deep of deep, where I forever long to be. Never let me go. Never leave. I will be, oh, I will be forever in glory.

Forever You are with me.

Where do you go when you are tired and weary? Where do you go when you are lost and scared? Where do you go when this whole world seems to be against you? Where do you go running and scared? Go enter into the presence of the King of Kings. Enter into the presence of the One who fulfills all your dreams. Enter into the presence of the One who loves and cares for you. Enter in, it's He who sees you through. Enter into the Father's open arms. Enter in and feel Him so strong. Enter in, He is inviting you. Enter in and believe in truth. Enter in, He is always right there. Enter in, there is no time to be scared. Enter in, your Father is waiting for you. Enter in and receive so much truth. Enter in, now is the time. Enter in, all is really fine. Enter into the deep of deep. Enter in child and believe. Enter in, His presence is here. Enter in and cast out your fear. Enter in, He is waiting for you. Enter in, it's the best thing you could ever do.

Enter into the deep loving presence of God.

Holy, holy is the One who comes to the cross to be undone. Lay your burdens there and see just how free you can be. We have a Savior who died for thee. Never let us forget the pain we did not see. For He came and He went to that cross so we could sit and worship Him at His feet. O Jesus, O Jesus, I believe You have died and rose again and took away our many sins. To say thank You could never be enough to love us no matter what. O Jesus, how we love and adore You. Jesus, O Jesus, come back soon.

> "Keep in mind that we who belong to Jesus, the Anointed One, have already experienced crucifixion. For everything connected with our self-life was put to death on the cross and crucified with Messiah" (Galatians 5:24, TPT).

Father, holy and pure. Your light shines through this cold dark world. Let us never dim Your light but forever be satisfied. This world will cut deep like a knife, but all is well, all is fine when I see my hope is secure in this faith I have. You came and endured to one day bring us home when we call on Your name and be enthroned. Father, O Father, hear me say, I love You for each and every day, but I will not miss this world we live in now. I will forever be high above the clouds, sitting and soaking in awe of You. O Father, Father please come back soon.

> "Then Jesus said, 'I am light to the world and those who embrace me will experience life-giving light, and they will never walk in darkness'" (John 8:12, TPT).

When we follow You, we see truth. When we obey, we feel peace. Please God, go before us and wipe out all our insecurities. May we sit and rest in Your will and tests. Many will come. Many will go. Lead us down the right road. May we look up and follow You there, and never look back into our cares. May we abide and trust in You. May we walk and see truth. You are the creator. You are all and all. You have us in the big and small, Abba. When tough times come, please come hold us through everyone.

> "Because God is your confidence in times of crisis, keeping your heart at rest in every situation" (Proverbs 3:26, TPT).

O Jesus, precious one. You came as a child to be undone, mistreated, mocked, bullied and tried. O Jesus, how You came alive to make us all see what life can truly be. Thank God, we did not miss. Thank God, He showed us this. A child was born to save us from sin, to one day be in heaven again. Oh, let us feel. Let us receive just what a precious gift this was to Thee. Let us honor You all our days and never forget those last days when You suffered and were beat. Oh, how the enemy loved his schemes. But only for a bit did he think he won, then You did what no one has done. You raised up from that tomb, and Father, O Father, we sure believe You all our days. We will tell and stay in Your truth, Lord, we sure love You.

> "And they will hand him over to the Romans to be mocked, tortured, and crucified. Yet three days later he will be raised to life again" (Matthew 20:19, TPT).

Persecution is intense. Persecution comes from many men. From many men who do not know. From many men who are called to show and attack what God gave you. To take what you have and stabs you. Persecution will rise in the end days to come. Persecution is set, but we have already won. The Man, the Man who took on sin. The Man, the Man who has called us to His plan was persecuted for the sake of you, was persecuted for his truth.

> "And the same persecutions and diffi-
> culties I have endured, you have also
> endured. Yes, you know all about what I
> had to suffer while in Antioch, Iconium,
> and Lystra. You're aware of all the per-
> secution I endured there; yet the Lord
> delivered me from every single one of
> them!" (2 Timothy 3:11, TPT).

Jesus, Jesus, precious Holy One. Jesus, Jesus, You are the only One who makes my heart love so deep. Jesus, O Jesus, I feel when You weep. Jesus, O Jesus, You are so kind. Jesus, O Jesus, and the best friend of mine. Jesus, O Jesus, I think of what I could've missed if I never said, I love You and You are worth all of it. Jesus, O Jesus, You chose me first. Jesus, O Jesus, that's my worth. Jesus, O Jesus, You are so kind. Jesus, O Jesus, forever mine.

> "For your heart will always pursue what you value as your treasure" (Matthew 6:21, TPT).

Where does our strength come from? Our hope, our security, our love, our faith, our ability to persevere through tragedy and trials. I believe it comes from one great almighty Father who looks down in awe and wonder of what He created. All His goodness wrapped up like a child easily given to us. Yes, given to us. Never shall we lose our trust in the One who gave it all. The One who knew no fault. Give it to Him. Give it to Him. Give it to Him. He will carry you along on eagles' wings. He will help you fly and dream. He will do it all without sting. He will show you everything. All the glory you could have just by never looking back but running into His arms. He will hold you tight. He's my everything. He's my right.

> "So trust in the Lord, all his people. For he is the only true hero, the wrap-around God who is our shield!" (Psalm 115:9, TPT).

The stillness of your breath. The stillness of your creation. The stillness of our Father bending down to whisper "everything is ok when you sit with me." Everything is peace when your eyes are on the unseen. Sit there now. Sit there. Bow to the King of all kings; to the Holy One who has come to bring us peace. Oh, the peace and joy we have when we lie there and be had by the One who knows and sees it all and is always there. Never too far. Seek the One there. Seek the One not your cares go there now and see as He sees. You go there now. There is so much truth. Stop the lies that come into your head. Lie down and be led. He makes a way when there is none. He plans and goes forth. It's all done.

Be still and soak in His presence.

Still waters run deep. They run with you and me. He has brought us here to dive in. Search no more. This is where you truly win. Still waters run deep. He has them for glory. Come dive in and seek the Kingdom. He has for our peace. Still waters run deep. He has them for you and me. Dive into the deep. That's where you find Him and receive.

Sit, seek, and receive all His glory.

This world is desperately crying out for attention. Missing links. Missing affection. If they fully grasped this one thing, it would change their lives in many ways. Watch what you say. Watch what you seek. This world is full of empty hope and dreams. Go to the One calling your name. Run to Him with no shame. He's waiting there for many to see. He is the only one who holds victory. Go there now. Seek Him and believe, He is the one holding heaven's keys.

> "So it is with your prayers. Ask and you'll receive. Seek and you'll discover. Knock on heaven's door, and it will one day open for you. Every persistent person will get what he asks for. Every persistent seeker will discover what he needs. And everyone who knocks persistently will one day find an open door" (Luke 11:9-10, TPT).

Letting go, so hard to do. Letting go can revive truth. Letting go is what He calls us to do. Letting go should be so easy but hard to do. What does letting go mean? What does letting go bring? The Father calls us to eternity; but letting go is a must to receive, to receive all the peace He is willing to give, all the peace so we can live so abundantly, wild, and free. So free, free to be what He has called us to be. So I may ask Lord, what does letting go do? I know it will honor and glorify truth. So, letting go I will do, as You took on the cross to hold our truth.

Take a deep breath and let go.

Where does this great love come from? How can you love so deep? How can You promise to always keep, always keep us in Your sight, always stay and never say goodbye? What kind of love is this? What kind of love stays and never misses? What kind of love do I deserve? What kind of love is heard? None like Yours. You are so true. None like Yours. It goes beyond the moon. Jesus, thank You for this love that wraps around the stars. Jesus, You are my true superstar. Jesus, You are holy and true. Jesus, I love You.

> "May the unconditional love of the Lord Jesus, the Anointed One, be with your spirit!" (Philemon 1:25, TPT).

Peace and joy in the trials of life brings our soul pure delight. When we let go and enter in the way Jesus wants us to live, turn away from anger and sin, let go, repent the joy of the Lord is our strength. When we let go, He is well pleased. Job well done, good and faithful servant. You are spiritually mature and ready to take the cold world. What they do and have done, you can walk through with eyes on the One who pressed on and endured all. Oh child, this is not how we have been called to slumber and sleep, to weep and stay depressed but to rise up with the best, perseverance, and truth. O Lord, how You show us Your heart when things get tough. Learn to start on a better path today. Leave the old ways to stray. The King of heaven is here to take all those burdens away. Walk away in peace. Walk away and believe. The thoughts that come from the enemy has to flee when we set our eyes on the King of Kings glory. May we fix our eyes on the glory of our King and release the burdens of everything. Do not conform to the patterns of this world, but be renewed, transformed by the One who created and remains in us all. Those that seek to believe His ways, His thoughts are higher than our earthly carnal fleshly desires. O Lord, when I get lost in the way, please draw me back. Renew this mind of Christ to walk and flow in Your every word. Father, You deserve all of us. All our best to live a life fully safe and secure in You and You alone. Not this dark cold world that leaves us anxious and stressed. Father, O Father, You know best. May we lay to rest all those earthly things that come between our hearts desires to be with Thee.

> "Stop imitating the ideals and opinions of the culture around you, but be inwardly transformed by the Holy Spirit through a total reformation of how you think. This will empower you to discern God's will as you live a beautiful life, satisfying and perfect in his eyes" (Romans 12:2, TPT).

When the days come and go, and you don't quite understand or know, reach out for His loving hand. Kindness, love, and truth will always be smiling back at you. Kindness, warmth, His touch will come down, and you feel nothing but love when these days seem long and hard. Reach up, He is loving, so strong. Let go of your worries and regret. Let go until there is nothing left. Let go. Look up to the One who sees. Let go and let all the rest be.

> "For he has conquered us with his great love and his kindness has melted our hearts. His faithfulness lasts forever and he will never fail you. So go ahead, let it all out! Praise Yah! O Yah!" (Psalm 117:2, TPT).

Lord, help us walk through the waiting. Well, help us see what others cannot tell. Help us let go and just have peace. Help us see there is more to dream. Don't let us sit and wait in our pit. Let us have hope. The only hope You give. We know You have come to give us life so free. Father, O Father, help us see, when we walk by faith and not by sight, we can walk through the darkest nights with so much joy and so much peace because I believe You have only the best for me.

> "He's the hope that holds me and the Stronghold to shelter me, the only God for me, and my great confidence" (Psalm 91:2, TPT).

Persecuted ones hold on. It's ok. Don't fight. It's won and all a good night when those persecutions come. Know the battle is already won. It was paid on Calvary. It was paid and hell was defeated. Oh, loved ones, know enemies will come and they will go. Hold on to truth. Hold on to our Father loving you. To be persecuted means you are gaining everything. The Kingdom is at hand, and you are a part of His plan. Take hope, take strides, leave the rest behind. It's His Kingdom at hand, and I'm all for His plan.

> "Have you endured all these trials and persecutions for nothing?" (Galatians 3:4, TPT).

When I come and let go, all is well with my soul. When I come and seek you, all is well and only for the few. The few who choose to love and see. The few who walk sparingly, counting the cost and saying yes. O Father, what could be better than this, when our eyes meet that day I could say, I lived fully for Your Kingdom and purpose and plan. O Father, help me see it all from Your hand. It is strong, mighty, loving too. Father, O Father, I simply adore You. See me now where I'm at. See me Father and that's a wrap. Come now, see me where I'm at. Come now, it's all Your plan.

Choose well. Count the cost. Say yes to the Father's plan that was bought.

Lord, as I sit here tonight, I think of all those who are not alright. As they walk this world hand and hand, do they ever look back and see You again? Are their thoughts on You or what this world offers? Are they reminded of the things that are not seen but dare to dream? Are they stuck in a rut when the going gets tough? Do they know how to go deep and surrender to Thee? Are they lost in a world where everything seems dim or will they be awakened by the light that burns within? As I see these people placed on my heart, Father, O Father, call them in for a brand-new start.

> "Let my passion for life be restored, tasting joy in every breakthrough you bring to me. Hold me close to you with a willing spirit that obeys whatever you say" (Psalm 51:12, TPT).

When you are hurting and lost, count the cost. Jesus walked and believed there is something greater than what we see. Have the faith. For one day when no more would be at loss or stray, have the hope that lives in you to come alive and pull you through. Go now and seek, the One who gives you peace. Go now, full of joy, that's His will to love and not destroy.

> "Until then, there are three things that remain: faith, hope, and love—yet love surpasses them all. So above all else, let love be the beautiful prize for which you run" (1 Corinthians 13:13, TPT).

Lord, what do you say about Pentecost? I say it is a holy, holy, holy, holy, holy, holy day. Let the angels sing. It is a holy, holy, holy, holy day. May my spirit fall on you, live in you, revive you, keep you, bless you, protect you, guide and honor you, fulfill you all your days. Now enjoy this gift I have given you. Run in it, have joy, love, peace, patience, kindness, goodness all your days and self-control that this world does not know. Now go out, I say go out. The signs, miracles, wonders, all come when the Holy Spirit falls upon. Believe them, see them, rejoice and be glad in them. This is the way your ministry should be, should lead with me, the Holy Spirit, living inside thee. Now go out, be about your Father's business and do not doubt what the Holy Spirit can do through you, through true. Go out wildflower, believe and endure. Go out with kindness on your heart forevermore. Go out, go out and truly see, this day of Pentecost is really me.

> "On the day Pentecost was being fulfilled, all the disciples were gathered in one place. Suddenly they heard the sound of a violent blast of wind rushing into the house from out of the heavenly realm. The roar of the wind was so overpowering it was all anyone could bear! Then all at

once a pillar of fire appeared before their eyes. It separated into tongues of fire that engulfed each one of them. They were all filled and equipped with the Holy Spirit and were inspired to speak in tongues— empowered by the Spirit to speak in languages they had never learned!" (Acts 2:1-4, TPT).

Father, You call us into the deep of deep. For when I'm here, I simply see, the beauty of Jesus smiling at me. Father, O Father, if I ever stray, wake me up and I will lie in my bow where my promises are sent. I will lie there still and never worry about the rent, as I know You take care of those flowers in the field. Surely You say You will take care of me here. Less I worry and sin no more, I see now heaven is holding the door.

> "And why would you worry about your clothing? Look at all the beautiful flowers of the field. They don't work or toil" (Matthew 6:28, TPT).

All who are lost will surely be found. Father, how could they stray and let You down? You have loved us from the beginning to the end. You have loved us, that was part of your plan. I pray everyone sees this love You have for me. It is better than my eyes have ever seen. My heart is full and pumping for more, for more, for more of heaven's doors. Open up wide and receive, receive, receive. This, Father, is everything to me.

> "But Christ proved God's passionate love for us by dying in our place while we were still lost and ungodly!" (Romans 5:8, TPT).

When you are tired, weary, and worn, look up child. He comes like a storm. He will come and rescue you. He will be there with truth. He will come into the deep of deep. Rest, oh rest, and believe He has come to see. To see us into heaven's eternity. Rest assured nothing will pass through His loving arms. Child, ask, ask oh ask, His precious heart. He will carry you through open and armed. Oh child, if you could see the power He holds, you would have the strength to carry on forevermore.

> "I know what it means to lack, and I know what it means to experience overwhelming abundance. For I'm trained in the secret of overcoming all things, whether in fullness or in hunger. And I find that the strength of Christ's explosive power infuses me to conquer every difficulty" (Philippians 4:12-13, TPT).

Mary, I come to you from God. Child you are well and highly favored. The angel said, "Mary you will have a child and you will name him Jesus and he will save the world". Mary, oh Mary, you are highly favored with our Lord. Mary, you will birth this heavenly masterpiece. Mary, oh Mary, how did you trust? Mary, how did you hold this baby? How, oh how, did you hold this miracle in your womb? Mary, oh Mary, how did you hold this miracle in your womb? Mary, oh Mary, oh Mary, do you truly know what you gave when you obeyed? Mary, oh Mary, you are such true love. We can see with your eyes. When we don't understand, we can see it's all part of the Lord's plan. Yes, yes, yes, I will say yes, yes, yes, Your will, Lord above ours. A King, a child was born. Oh, how this child was born and so adorned.

Yes, Lord, yes. Whatever Your will is, You have my yes.

Rest and restore. Rest and restore. You gave us so much more, rest and restore. Rest and restore. Lay down life's burdens and soar. Rest and restore. Rest and restore. He has called us to rest and roar.

> "Simply join your life with mine. Learn my ways and you'll discover that I'm gentle, humble, easy to please. You will find refreshment and rest in me" (Matthew 11:29, TPT).

All day long, I sit and pray. All day long, I yield to faith. All day long, I cast him out. All day long, I know what You are about. All day long, I seek Your dreams, Your dreams for me, Your dreams to lead. Father, oh never will I lose my grip, for You are life and I won't miss.

> "What joy overwhelms everyone who keeps the ways of God, those who seek him as their heart's passion!" (Psalm 119:2, TPT).

If I wanted to tell the world anything, it would be one thing, one thing alone. This life that you live is not your own. When you give up your life for the One who has given it to you, oh how sweet, oh sweet this will be to you. This life that we live is not our own. Jesus died to give us so much more. Don't place your treasures in this dark world, place them in heaven where you could live forevermore.

> "For God's call on our lives is not to a life of compromise and perversion but to a life surrounded in holiness" (1 Thessalonians 4:7, TPT).

Where does the time go? It comes and it goes. Most of the things stay the same, but some will be different and change. What do we do with our time? Is it spent on our own fleshly desires to please people? Or a surrender to please God? Time will come and go, but His love remains and always will. So, seek him first, be with Him always. And always, always do His will because what we know about time is that it will come and it will go, and we always want to be in the will of our Heavenly Father and know.

> "So we proclaim to you what we have seen and heard about this Life-Giver so that we may share and enjoy this life together. For truly our fellowship is with the Father and with his Son, Jesus, the Anointed One" (1 John 1:3, TPT).

Sometimes when I need a quiet moment, I speak, Jesus, O Jesus, just come to me. I don't understand, I don't know what to do. Jesus, would you come so I can follow You? With everything I know, with everything I am, Jesus, all I want is your plan.

> "Then he said to me, 'The God of our ancestors has destined you to know his plan and for you to see the Holy One and to hear his voice" (Acts 22:14, TPT).

The wind, the waves, the seas, compares nothing to His glory. So majestic and true, Jesus, let my life always honor You. So holy and pure, You are forevermore. Keep me in this safe place and be forever my eternity.

> "And he has entered once and forever into the Holiest Sanctuary of All, not with the blood of animal sacrifices, but the sacred blood of his own sacrifice. And he alone has made our salvation secure forever!" (Hebrews 9:12, TPT).

This creation, the beauty that we see now compares nothing to eternity. The water, the trees, take them in and breathe; it compares nothing to eternity set before us. Enjoy all He has set before. One day, it will be even more glorious.

> "Everything he does is full of splendor and beauty! Each miracle demonstrates his eternal perfection" (Psalm 111:3, TPT).

My heart, my heart is set apart. My heart, my heart was Yours from the start. You formed me in my mother's womb. You formed me knowing I would honor You. You formed me, and now I see You formed, oh how could this be? You formed and now all my dreams are for one day to be with You for eternity.

> "You formed my innermost being, shaping my delicate inside and my intricate outside, and wove them all together in my mother's womb" (Psalm 139:13, TPT).

Adoration. Worship the Lord only! High praises to Him. Seek Him whole heartedly. Bow down and worship Him. Adore Him and His faithfulness.

> "Yours, O LORD, is the greatness and the power and the glory and the victory and the majesty, indeed everything that is in the heavens and on the earth; Yours is the dominion and kingdom, O LORD, and You exalt Yourself as head over all" (1 Chronicles 29:11, AMP).

Close your eyes child, and rest. Close your eyes and see the best. Close your eyes, the peace it brings when you are walking with Thee. Close your eyes for a minute now, close your eyes and learn to bow. To yield your heart and mind to Him, close your eyes and reap the gem.

> "My son, give me your heart and let your eyes delight in my ways" (Proverbs 23:26, AMP).

When you get hurt remember, the enemy comes for your worth. Smile child and know, when persecution comes it's because you are in the know. Keep walking and staying true. This shall pass and all the honor holds true. In this life, people will come against, but we can choose to forgive offense.

> "For all who choose to live godly as worshipers of Jesus, the Anointed One, will also experience persecution" (2 Timothy 3:12, TPT).

With all life's ups and downs, what crown shall be? What crown do you seek? The world's or eternity? In the final days to come, don't be the one sitting on the sideline watching. Be the won called to win

> "Blessed [happy, spiritually prosperous, favored by God] is the man who is steadfast under trial and perseveres when tempted; for when he has passed the test and been approved, he will receive the [victor's] crown of life which the Lord has promised to those who love Him" (James 1:12, AMP).

Mary did you know what you said yes to? Mary did you know you would birth and hold our Savior? Mary did you know the world would not accept and enter Him in? Mary did you know He would save us all? Mary did you know He would die on that cross an awful death for us to live? Mary did you know what yes meant? Did you really, really know what your yes meant? Mary did you know? Mary, thank you for your yes. Thank you for bringing our savior into this world and saying yes. Thank you, Mary, for saying yes.

> "Then Mary responded, saying, "This is amazing! I will be a mother for the Lord! As his servant, I accept whatever he has for me. May everything you have told me come to pass." And the angel left her" (Luke 1:38, TPT).

I think about my past and look back. It seemed so long ago, I was on that dark lonely road, filling my fleshly desires but never really full. There was always a void until I met Jesus. He took all those desires away and gave me new ones to stay. Now I'm full of life and love, and nothing compares to His cup.

> "Create a new, clean heart within me. Fill me with pure thoughts and holy desires, ready to please you" (Psalm 51:10, TPT).

Another thing would be, don't go another day from your knees, your knees, your knees. Oh, seek the King, the King of everything. For on my knees, I found Him there, for on my knees, everything was more clear. For on my knees, oh if you could see, for on my knees, how truly He showed me. He showed me love. He showed me grace. He showed me everything at the sound of His name. That quiet time you can never replace. He will show you more in a minute then you could see in a day.

> "At each and every sunrise you will hear my voice as I prepare my sacrifice of prayer to you. Every morning I lay out the pieces of my life on the altar and wait for your fire to fall upon my heart" (Psalm 5:3, TPT).

If I were to write a book, I would say Jesus' letters have gotten me through all these days. These days, these days have come and gone, and I would not have survived without them. These letters, these letters are life to me, oh Jesus' lovers can't you see? When you give up your life and truly seek, He will give you even more than you dare to dream.

> "As a result of our ministry, you are living letters written by Christ, not with ink but by the Spirit of the living God—not carved onto stone tablets but on the tablets of tender hearts" (2 Corinthians 3:3, TPT).

I remember how hard it was to give that old life to You. I remember how lonely I felt walking without You. So, I chose that day to leave the old astray, and for that I have seen the light in a whole new way.

> "You who spend your days shrouded in darkness can now say, "We have seen a brilliant Light." And those who live in the dark shadow land of death can now say, "The Dawning Light arises on us" (Matthew 4:16, TPT).

With all that I am, with all that I do, Jesus, O Jesus, let me show You, how I am so true. I want to show You by the fruits that I bear, I want to show You when someone comes against me and I don't care. I want to show You what You mean to me, I want to show You please, please, please. I want to show You my heart is set apart, I want to show You, please let me start. I want to show You everything You are to me; I want to show You. Please Jesus, show me.

> "But he answered me, 'My grace is always more than enough for you, and my power finds its full expression through your weakness.' So I will celebrate my weaknesses, for when I'm weak I sense more deeply the mighty power of Christ living in me" (2 Corinthians 12:9, TPT).

Water we drink, water we thirst. It all comes to pass with a burst. A burst of truth, a burst of You. A burst, a mist of a cure longing for You. Sit here with me, sit here and be, sit here and lead us into victory. Sit here and see, sit here and be, sit here and lead us into sweet victory. It's You we seek. It's You we thirst. It's You, only You, as we burst. Send us Your spirit every second of the day, send us, never leave us to stray. It's You we see. It's You we thirst. It's your presence we feel with a burst. Thank You, Jesus, for Your fresh outpour. Fill us up, we need You more.

> "Now I'm reaching out to you, thirsting for you like the dry, cracked ground thirsts for rain. Pause in his presence" (Psalm 143:6, TPT).

I often think, why do people stray? I often think, it's not ok. I often think, this one day. I often think, hey, hey, hey. I often think, but what does thinking do? I often think, I want to please You. I often think of many things, but at the end of the day, I lay, lay, lay and say, what does mere thoughts say? It's our actions we pray.

> "'For My thoughts are not your thoughts,
> Nor are your ways My ways,' declares the
> LORD" (Isaiah 55:8, AMP).

Oh healing, I ask, I ask of You a lot. Oh healing, You say was paid and bought. Oh healing, Your words speak true. Oh healing, I know You are You. Healing is healing in the know. Healing, oh healing, how You show healing. How I could be healed from head to toe. Healing comes and healing shows.

> "Then Jesus said to her, 'Daughter, because you dared to believe, your faith has healed you. Go with peace in your heart, and be free from your suffering!'" (Mark 5:34, TPT).

Lying down on green pasture you say laying there, I love to pray, pray, pray. Oh, the delight and glory one day that I get to see my loving Father face to face. That day could come right now, and you would find me in my bow, worshiping in awe of You. O Jesus, O Father, please come soon.

> "Come and kneel before this Creator-God; come and bow before the mighty God, our majestic maker!" (Psalm 95:6, TPT).

When we go through hard times, we have a choice to see the good, the bad, or the ugly. Lord, let us choose the good. We know all things are made for the good of those who love You. We will walk in obedience to the calling on our life, and will always say yes, with faith and trust, as You walk with us in those hard seasons, where we will grow, persevere, and be even more molded into the image of our creator. Thank you for the hard, for we know as we walk through fire, we will be forged to be more like our savior, our precious one we adore and love.

> "Honor God's holy instructions and life will go well for you. But if you despise his ways and choose your own plans, you will die" (Proverbs 19:16, TPT).

I look around and You are not there. I sit with all these cares. Search my heart, Lord, and see if there is anything blocking You and me. Search it, Lord, take every thought. Make it obey the truth You taught. Go before me now as I wait and see that heaven's gates are wide open for all this glory, raining down on me. O Father, I plead, make us right, make me whole, this my Father is all I know.

> "Jesus continued, 'It has been written by the prophets, "They will all be taught by God himself." If you are really listening to the Father and learning directly from him, you will come to me'" (John 6:45, TPT).

Lord, I love you so, I can't fathom. You built our home with such love and majesty, Father, O Father, please, please, please, come show me the way, show me the light, I want to live fully in Your delight. May I always honor, obey and love You; may You always see me as true. Father, my only hope is one day I will see what it's like to be living in eternity where You are and always will be. Father, O Father, please take me there with Thee.

> "My Father's house has many dwelling places. If it were otherwise, I would tell you plainly, because I go to prepare a place for you to rest" (John 14:2, TPT).

The Lord teaches us to cut off anything that is not life. Cut it off, remain in the vine. Be pruned to bear fruit, the fruit of the spirit that brings life and joy abundantly. Bear so much fruit, bear fruit so much fruit. This will take cutting out the sin of the world and remain fastened, locked in, with our savior, Lord. Bear fruit, He commands, bear so much fruit and see how it effects life, how it affects thee. Cut the sin out, cut it out now, and return to your first love, your only love. Repent. Go into the deep of deep, and child, reap, reap, reap.

> "I am the sprouting vine and you're my branches. As you live in union with me as your source, fruitfulness will stream from within you—but when you live separated from me you are powerless" (John 15:5, TPT).

Love comes. You see love was nailed to a tree. Love was for you and me. Love comes. You see love comes in the midnight air. Love comes when you do not care. Love comes for all to see. Love comes. Oh, how could this be, this love, this love You have for me. This love, this love is truly one to be. This love, this love, all this love, could go to the depths and still run, run, run. This love, this love rings so true. This love, this love I have for You. This love You give, and I receive. This love, this love, oh, how could it be.

> "But God clearly shows and proves His own love for us, by the fact that while we were still sinners, Christ died for us" (Romans 5:8, AMP).

Persecution, jealousy, sly remarks, all come and hit you from the dark. Lord, help us focus our eyes on You. Help us to see You are truth. What others may say, what others will do, is no representation of You. Seek love above all things, seek joy and let freedom ring. For we will not conform to the ways of this world, we will look up and truly soar.

> "O our God, will You not judge them? For we are powerless against this great multitude which is coming against us. We do not know what to do, but our eyes are on You" (2 Chronicles 20:12, AMP).

My thoughts take hold and run to a place unknown. My thoughts take hold and run to a place unknown. When I cast them down, they come back revengefully being found. When I cast them down, they wreak havoc to come so near. When I cast them down all hell breaks loose, but when I cast them down and choose not to lose. I battle with right from wrong, they come in so strong. But when I declare the battle is won, I take a deep breath and hold on and remember the verse that says make our minds to obey Christ, and it becomes way more clear for me. The enemy is out to take me down. He comes in my thoughts but can't stick around because I have a Father who won that go round.

> "So keep your thoughts continually fixed on all that is authentic and real, honorable and admirable, beautiful and respectful, pure and holy, merciful and kind. And fasten your thoughts on every glorious work of God, praising him always" (Philippians 4:8, TPT).

Miracles, miracles, miracles, are everywhere. Open your eyes, they are in the air. Jesus came to set us free, that's a miracle don't you believe? Miracles, miracles are everywhere, Jesus gives them and takes away our cares. Nothing too big or too small, miracles are here when you call. Precious Jesus, You have shown miracles. Precious Jesus, let us never grow cold to these everyday miracles. Precious Jesus, You have come to show. Precious Jesus, miracles You hold.

> "Yes, he did mighty miracles, and we are overjoyed!" (Psalm 126:3, TPT).

Be present in today, in faith, hope, love and joy. Be present in today, every day, every day, every day, every day. Every day is a gift, every day is a gift. Jesus is our miracle today. Every day, He is our miracle, He is our miracle, He is our miracle. Jesus' birth is one of the first miracles and the most amazing miracle. Immanuel, God with us, Immanuel, God with us, Immanuel, God with us. Jesus. We trust in Jesus. We trust in Jesus. We trust in Jesus. We trust in Jesus. We trust in Jesus. We trust in Jesus. We trust in Jesus. We trust, holy, holy, holy King of Kings. We trust, holy, holy, holy, You are so worthy and true. Our only pure sacred adoration is for You. Eyes have not seen, ears have not heard, this perfect glory found in our Lord. Eyes have not seen, ears have not heard, glory, glory for You our Lord.

> "Glory to God in the highest [heaven], And on earth peace among men with whom He is well-pleased" (Luke 2:14, AMP).

Why do we sin? Do we take our focus on the will of our Father, and replace it with the world and our own fleshy desire? Take back, take back, take back. Be holy. Repent. Change from your evil ways. Seek the Lord above and soar in a life full of love. Sin is death. Jesus is life. Trade the darkness for the light. Seek Him now, toss the sin out. Child toss it out and run to the Father. The only One who holds life, our precious life, filled by the Holy Ghost. The One who loves us most.

> "And now you must repent and turn back
> to God so that your sins will be removed,
> and so that times of refreshing will stream
> from the Lord's presence" (Acts 3:19,
> TPT).

Lord, when we journey through life let us surrender for You to guide. Your will, your way, may we always pray. As we journey through life, give us eyes to see, grace to live, ears to hear, a heart to love, hands to serve, and Your true words to share. To be one with Thee. Help us Lord. Lead us, help us see, we live to serve only Thee.

> "Serve and worship the awe-inspiring God. Recognize his greatness and bow before him, trembling with reverence in his presence" (Psalm 2:11, TPT).

Christmas. Christ is born. Christmas. A child adorned. Christmas is so many things. Christmas, do you hear the ring? Christmas has come, and I have spent this Christmas sitting with Him. Christmas, what a magical day. Christmas. Jesus, you were born in the hay. Christmas. Jesus, we hold so dear. Christmas. My joy and sweet tears. Christmas, what love it brings. Christmas. You came.

A kiss from heaven came down on Christmas Day.

Adoration, preference to yield. To surrender, to worship the King of Kings, who came as a baby to save us from our enemies. Jesus, O Jesus, our eyes fixed on these things You have given us. You are so holy and true, all our adorations for You and only You. King of Kings, Holy of Holies, You are highly exalted above all. Happy, happy, happy birthday Jesus. We love You, honor, and only seek Your presence of the one adorned.

> "And so the Living Expression became a man and lived among us! And we gazed upon the splendor of his glory, the glory of the One and Only who came from the Father overflowing with tender mercy and truth!" (John 1:14, TPT).

Patience, patience, patience, I ask. I feel it may be the hardest of tasks. All day long I seek Your strength, but something hits and steals my peace. Lord, give me patience and the strength to know, it's Your key that holds patience. I need the fruit we all love to bear. The fruit, the fruit that endures and makes us strong. Your patience, Father, I seek Your patience. I ask Your patience I will keep.

> "For you know that when your faith is tested it stirs up power within you to endure all things" (James 1:3, TPT)

Immanuel, God is with us. Immanuel, love so true. Immanuel, God is with us. What joy and peace it brings to believe Immanuel is a spring, a river flowing through our joints, our hearts aligned with truth. Immanuel brings me peace, brings me love, and more great things. Immanuel, when I sleep, Immanuel, when I dream. Immanuel, how precious is Your name? Immanuel, You are my deepest strength. Immanuel, You are everything to me. Immanuel, You bring me joy abundantly. Immanuel, You will never leave. Immanuel, it's You I seek.

> "Grace, mercy, and peace (inner calm, a sense of spiritual well-being) will be with us, from God the Father and from Jesus Christ, the Father's Son, in truth and love" (2 John 1:3, AMP).

Bless them, bless them, I hear him say. When they come against and try to take your praise. Bless them and let them be. Your joy and strength will be your victory.

Bless your enemies at all times.

Jesus Your power. Jesus Your strength. Jesus Your book, Your heart You speak. Jesus You are kind. Jesus You are well. Jesus it's Your story I shall tell! The end, Amen.

About the Author

I believe it's the Father, the Son, and the Holy Ghost, and everything else flows from it. I have a wonderful husband, Justin, of fourteen years and two beautiful daughters, Addie, 12, and Liv. 7. We reside in Bourbon, MO and just started a ministry Jesus gave us in 2019, called True Love Ministries. My heart is to flow from the heart of Jesus and tell the world the relationship with Jesus is the most important one you will ever have. Keep it holy, keep it safe, and make time in the secret place. He will show you in one minute what you couldn't find in a lifetime without Him. God Bless, and I hope these prayers touch your heart as they have touched mine.

Lacey Whittaker

CPSIA information can be obtained
at www.ICGtesting.com
Printed in the USA
BVHW030025250421
605795BV00015B/137